BETTA FISH
AND BACKCOUNTRY

Nicholas Trieste

Betta Fish and Backcountry

Nicholastrieste.com

Leave feedback at:
Nicholastrieste@gmail.com
Twitter: @nicholastrieste
Instagram: @nicholastrieste

ISBN-13: 978-1-7342915-1-3

First Edition

Printed in the U.S.A.

For Richard Arthur Turner III

I wish we could have had a moment together to say I love you, instead of the silence which pervaded our relationship.

FOREWORD

I've done at least four re-writes on this, trying to balance honesty without overwriting it. The loss of my father in 2017 set everything in motion. This all started as a poetry collection, and quickly evolved into a travel prose and poetry collection, but even I think that falls flat. At times, re-reading this feels more of a memoir to me. All of the travel and writing was a way to cope with loss. My dad and I didn't have the best relationship, and he passed away suddenly while we were in the middle of not speaking. His death led to a lot of soul-searching, a lot of traveling, and a lot of isolation. I think it was the best thing for me to take years to myself, and look for what made me happy, instead of continuing to frequent local bars, and go in and out of toxic relationships. I've grown, I think, from everything and have (mostly) come to terms with my dad's passing. Some days are better than others. He struggled with addiction for years, and was actually clean when he died, though I never believed him; I had heard the story before—over ten years of the same thing. If him and I could talk, we would have a long conversation.

I've been nothing but blessed after I decided to take on all of these travel adventures. From the mountains and glaciers of Alaska where I fell, and ruined parts of my body, to the white roads of Texas where I drove muscle cars to relive his drag racing days; the sweltering bayou of Louisiana, I chased love down there; I hid in the waters of Washington, kayaking with the seals on the border of Canada, hiking Rainier, and debating if I should run from my life and everyone I ever knew; the South-West was to push myself to the limit in the desert heat. I'd get lost in the canyons and completely came to terms with the very real possibility that I might die. I went to Yosemite to see the legend of El Capitan, and hike Half-Dome: that was the hardest thing I've ever done. I'd tell my dad all about these trips, and the things he never was able to do due to his broken back. I like to believe he came with me while I got away from civilization. It's a comforting thought: that he was accompanying me and seeing all the beautiful wonders most people take for granted. This collection of poetry, prose, and self-philosophy came from all of this, if only for my own sanity. There's moments in here I've never said out loud, and the first time anyone will ever read them.

I don't know how to describe some emotions or what it's like to lose a parent young, when you're so ill-equipped to handle it. I don't think we're ever equipped to handle it no matter how good or bad our relationships with our parents are.

So Dad, if you're really out there, and reading this, I hope you've enjoyed the journey as much as I have. This next one is for you.

October 2019

Nicholas Trieste

It feels like the gray chapter of my life
has just begun

Betta Fish and Backcountry

I remember the exact way my father's apartment was set up. There was a bucket of blood next to his disheveled bed from the blood transfusions that failed to work. They bled until he threw up and eventually died in bed, his pillows and blankets stained with bile, and nicotine. In his refrigerator there was an order of spaghetti and meatballs in a silver tray from the pizzeria close to his home. His closet held a small RC drone, and a brand-new pair of black dad shoes—you know the kind—the ones that have Velcro instead of laces. His pink iPhone 5 lay on the counter at 96%. He had a betta fish swimming around on his dresser that was covered in cigarette ashes.

I think he had gotten home from getting food, felt unwell, put his dinner away, left his phone on the counter, and went to lay in bed after grabbing a bucket, throwing up until those last moments washed over him January 24, 2017.

Nicholas Trieste

The sun won't shine today.

Betta Fish and Backcountry

See our breath as whispers on the morning
air

Words we're too afraid to say out loud

Nicholas Trieste

"dew"

Flowers of light
through window panes.
Cardinal-red,
Iridescent peacock,
And cherry blossom pink
Circling overhead.

Betta Fish and Backcountry

"The Last Outdoor Generation"

hot asphalt summers
where our feet burned on the sand beaches
while waiting on line
for frozen lemonades,
making bets on who could drink the most
without getting a brain freeze,
the ultimate competition,
a bluff of masculinity
among the salt stained air
and children laughing
to boomboxes their parents brought
for company to their towels
and shitty romance novels.

Nicholas Trieste

"Do not feed the wildlife"

Men and women
with cankles larger than redwoods
wrapped in white socks ripping at the
seams,
corpulent necks
marked by sunburn,
like wild raspberries.
Tourists swinging selfie sticks:
reeds in the wind,
or swords for attacking strangers,
a great way to practice my evasion
techniques while hiking.
Children stampeding the cliffsides
in a race to the bottom,
pushing through people
then off trail to destroy the fragile
vegetation,
footprints and sprained ankles left in
their wake.
Boomers in motorized wheelchairs
berating park rangers,
making demands that natural trails
be leveled and paved
for easy access,
complaining the wilderness isn't family
friendly
for their photo albums.

Betta Fish and Backcountry

None of this is life: it's an escapist reality of inconsequential meandering, and discourse. This has turned into a race to the bottom, piled high with debt to prove who has the most pristine fake-life. Where social interactions permutate and dissolve into nonsensical whimsies for recording on social apps. The addiction has started and when the supply is taken away, society as we all know it will deteriorate on a rapid scale never before seen in history: not by any of the infamous empires. Globalism and interconnectedness through technology has proven to be anti-humanitarian. I wish we could all see and agree on that, if only to limit the negative factors of where we are heading, and promote the positive ones.

Nicholas Trieste

morning fog rolled out on pines
crisp air flush against skin
steam rises from a mug
i run droplets of grass-dew through my
fingers
as the silent world goes by

Betta Fish and Backcountry

i want
a leather chair
smooth jazz
the smell of vanilla cigars
warm coffee
and your company

"Please respond"

Wordless,
Unbound,
Traveling among the stars.
Can you hear me?

Betta Fish and Backcountry

I'm reaching for stars buried in sand

Nicholas Trieste

I'd trade it all if only for more time

Betta Fish and Backcountry

do you shine
or take photos to seem like you do?

Nicholas Trieste

I promise all the time
you put into other people
would be better spent
on yourself.

Betta Fish and Backcountry

"A Haiku Of Me Trying To Remember The
Sound Of My Father"

i no longer hear
your voice in the silent space
between song lyrics

"Rialto"

The waves crash against the shore
Made of rocks

A dead seal with claw marks from a bear
Lay on the great expanse where the pines
Meet the beach

I'll make camp here
Listen to the conversation between the
sea
And the immensity jutting in the distance
Monuments of old giants

Betta Fish and Backcountry

I feel like I've wasted so much out here in Washington. I know how little I actually need to get through the day. Learning experience. I don't need things, or stuff. I just need water, food, pens and notebooks. It's all a waste. Everything. Only to exist for the world to see us.

Nicholas Trieste

The most comfortable and happiest I've been living on the edge of society, able to come and go as I please: disappear into the Olympic trees. It's getting cold now. I should sleep.

Betta Fish and Backcountry

Unutterable loneliness
wandering out here
in the canyons.
The loathsome mid-west
sand creeping in between
the cracks of my raw skin:
wallpaper peeling away
from an old home.

Nicholas Trieste

Thunderheads
Sunlight peeking through cracks in the
sky
Phosphorescence against a dull background
Lighting up the mundane

Betta Fish and Backcountry

The reflexive light drifts though noon
Perspiration on my forehead dreams of the
coming snow

Nicholas Trieste

"While drinking coffee at 3am looking at
the moon"

Everyone wants you to be honest about
your emotions
Until you're honest

Betta Fish and Backcountry

December 27, 2016, my birthday: the last day we ever spoke. Argued. Hanging up angrily, not wanting to speak to each other. And we never did. Four weeks later, to the day, you died. I'm sitting here on the first ridge of Mount Rainier, 11,000 feet up, thinking about my guilt: wanting to run away from my own life.

Nicholas Trieste

Some live lives like winter cardinals

Others like summer fireflies

Betta Fish and Backcountry

If you do something
Wrong
Enough times
It becomes your style

Nicholas Trieste

The wind has stopped

Betta Fish and Backcountry

"The Wake-dream"

Most days I believe myself
to be somewhere else
observing fauna
as they saunter through open fields
traversing canyons
littered with spines of monsters.
Anywhere but here

Nicholas Trieste

"A view of my kitchen window"

Streaks of light through a canopy
Dust motes dancing in the fog

Betta Fish and Backcountry

The sun is a pervert
watching people through white blinds.

Nicholas Trieste

Staring at the sun through thick clouds
A white orb in the sky
Burn out my fucking eyes
Please.

"Art Opening"

If I could
Paint
My body the color of
My sins
I'd leave out yellow

Nicholas Trieste

Last time I saw you, you weighed less
than I did. Your clothes. Barely clung to
your skin. There were patches on your
head where your hair used to be. You
tried to cover it all up with the hat I
now keep in my living room.

Betta Fish and Backcountry

"An old love letter"

she is the ocean
i'm lost at sea

Nicholas Trieste

"Sepia-colored memories"

remember all the promises you made
when you were in love?

"escape"

I write not to feel everything
;
I write to not feel anything

Nicholas Trieste

"heuristic"

i am human:
full of hell
—searching for heaven.

Betta Fish and Backcountry

Today I was able to see one of the last California condors as it wheeled and spun along the face of Angel's Landing in Zion National Park. Black against the dull-red and burnt-orange stone with white under its wings. While those around me sat and toyed with their phones, I watched it glide: a kite on the wind. Children from some camp yelled in the background, and tried to wrestle at the first landing. I didn't tell any of them what I was watching as I found a quiet corner through a cluster of desert shrubs. There was an old man and woman, still trying to keep young, sitting and enjoying the solitude. The chanting of conversation had turned into a low buzz of background noise. They said, "Hello," and asked if I was trying to get away from the crowds before I went up the chains with the thousand-foot drop on either side. I told them I was, and pointed overhead at the condor still circling, as if finding enjoyment in the incessant madness of being. They gazed with me, mouths open, as one of the last of a species went about living, maybe trying to teach a lesson, or provide a sign for those who cared to look up. We chose not to speak and only after it disappeared did any of us realize that

there were people around, still playing,
focused on things not nearly as important
as seeing the last of something pass on
the wind.

Betta Fish and Backcountry

"Irish mornings"

You waited tables
And when you left
The only company
At ours
Was whiskey
And black coffee

Nicholas Trieste

"A social commentary"

Bless us with sight
and
give us eyes to see.

Betta Fish and Backcountry

"Empty and we do not wake"

I loved those tiny little lights
Guides in the dark
North Stars of the dream

Nicholas Trieste

"Half-eaten apple in the Utah desert"

Someone put the sticker back on
Curled at both ends—
It barely clings to the glossy red skin
Pockmarked with brown fingernail
indentations.
The core still white-yellow:
Hints of decay only beginning to form.
The land stretches on for miles;
Grotesque yellow sand
Littered with greasewood:
In-grown hairs on a shaved head.

Betta Fish and Backcountry

"I struggle often"

"gone"

we are only
memories refracted
through words
of people
who never knew us.

Betta Fish and Backcountry

"betta fish and model cars"

i have flashes of memories with you
growing up,
showing me all the things I thought
you wanted to be my hobbies.

after you died,
i went through your boxes and journals
after years of us not speaking.

dad,
i think i understand you more now
than when you were alive;
you wanted to be all the things
you missed out on as a kid.

"Anacortes"

let my bones lie here:
forgotten even by god.

Betta Fish and Backcountry

"It started with 'Desperato'"

I went through your mountain
Of notebooks
Picked a piece of paper off my carpet
Labeled
"Songs to play at my funeral."

A tiny scrap
Overlooked by everyone
Filled with rock ballads
And 80's electronic music.

I've memorized all of the songs
You wanted to die to.

Nicholas Trieste

"Melancholia"

Instead of giving it away
I kept it—
swallowed the sun
to burn bright from the inside.

Betta Fish and Backcountry

"amazing grace"

My lungs are sulfur.
She sings into my ear
As I push my palms to my eyes.
I want the images to go away.

Some days I see the shadow out
Of the corner of my eye,
Swear I can catch her voice
On the wind.

Nicholas Trieste

"The social society"

Too old to explore the seas
And find new land;
Too young to traverse the stars
And find new homes—
The miserable middle ground
Of complacency.

Betta Fish and Backcountry

To travel with my tent has become home; New York is second. I exist there only during an interim, plotting trails I've never trekked as the sun starts to rise on new days. So starts a life of adventure.

Nicholas Trieste

"Winter comes and night unfolds"

the lows are getting lower
have i ever felt the sun

Betta Fish and Backcountry

"A letter to my father (apology)"

I hope there's a heaven
so I can imagine you able to
run again—
your mother in the distance
waiting with open arms
surrounded by the love
you wish we gave you.

Nicholas Trieste

"repetition"

maybe
the thing i've always
needed
was to become
insane

Betta Fish and Backcountry

social isolation for the sake of art

Nicholas Trieste

recluse
like deer in winter

Betta Fish and Backcountry

"If there is mirth and songs fill the air"

am i a cool breeze
or the torrents
which silence the birds?

Nicholas Trieste

"Realism"

I jump for joy
For only a moment
Then
I come back down

Betta Fish and Backcountry

"Everything about her was poetry"

The way her lips curled in when she
laughed
Her left foot tapping the floor while she
answered emails

Nicholas Trieste

i see it i see it!
out there on the sand
through a rhythmic haze,
undulating dunes—
the sound of water
—time spilling

Betta Fish and Backcountry

"1960"

Hand out the window of your car
Like an old movie
Loaded with film grain
Driving down a lone stretch of road
Maybe you'd be in love
Or running away from your past

Nicholas Trieste

It took a lot of falling apart
To know what I needed
And wanted

Betta Fish and Backcountry

I'll take nights alone
In a tent under the stars
Before I commit to someone
Who doesn't see me as a person

Nicholas Trieste

"Romance"

The wood splinters and fills the air
As the bonfire continues to burn.
Smoke dries out the eyes—
Stars overhead.
Wind brushes against the leaves
A lover
Treading familiar territory.

Betta Fish and Backcountry

"we ran."

The sky was pissing rain,
humidity suffocated our lungs,
made sweat feel heavy,
hair matted and pressed to our foreheads
like the fall leaves we used to collect,
press into books,
memories for the future we'd pretend
we had together.

"a place in history"

i wandered
seemingly lost amongst the sand and
sprouts of foliage,
ingrown hairs on a yellow landscape,
hoping for the shake of a snake's tail
or a black-winged bird to swoop down
and pick at the dead antelope smelling of
iron:
an open sewer in the city.

i wandered
to discover the right words
hidden in the sandstone,
red and orange
like a child's drawing of the sun—
to find them plastered on the cliff face,
a small kernel for the prospector;
searching for the feeling when it all
comes together:
that ineffable truth.

i wandered
and wondered
what if i run out of words—
what then?
do i dwindle,
a shadow lost to the sunset?
collapse like a star?
a point of existence glossed over.

Betta Fish and Backcountry

the clouds against the sky
milk poured into fresh coffee

Nicholas Trieste

Half Dome Cables

And I watched the world go by,
silent as we trundled up the lines. I sit
here as the sun passes, blaring through
clouds; wind whipping as ambient noise.
Beneath my feet, nothing but the sheer
cliffs to certain doom. I am terrified
and exhilarated all the same.

Betta Fish and Backcountry

Could you capture a perfect moment?
Her hair
Gilded
Reflecting the sun creeping through the
window,
A thief.
Outside a glacial morning,
Dew on the ground,
Tears of angels
Who cried through the night,
Crystallizing
And refracting light—
Rainbows of color if you looked hard
enough.
You see your breath on the wind,
The creation of clouds,
Heavy
That it almost hangs
Long enough to produce snow.
Your hands warmed
By a metallic camping mug,
White-knuckled,
Steam rising
Mixes with the wishes from your mouth
That this moment lasts forever.

Nicholas Trieste

"Neo New York at Twilight"

In alleys of flamingo lights
And sapphire neons,
We watched the homeless:
Transitory tourists
Vacationing
In the third world country
Of our own city.
Sweat pooled on the crooks of our noses,
Old rain on leaves now extinct.
In the bayou-humidity of mid-July
We watched peddlers trying to turn
Water into wine,
On a street lined with human shit
And fluorescent piss
Instead of gold.

Betta Fish and Backcountry

"My father's a stranger"

My father's a stranger
Defined in newspaper clippings:
A black uniform
Next to a woman
And a burned down house.

My father's a stranger,
Love letters held by bubblegum rubber
bands
In a box in my living room
Tell me
Of women who loved him before my mother.

My father's a stranger
Remembered by drag racing trophies
Flooring a crimson 1989 mustang GT
Pouring bagged ice onto the engine block
After winning.

My father's a stranger
His last mesh hat stained by nicotine
In a zip-lock bag
Still smelling of Newports.

My father's a stranger
Ashes on his mother's grave
Which i spread
On the only cold day June ever had.

Nicholas Trieste

Let me sit here
Watch the sun rise in silence
Even the wind keeps quiet

Betta Fish and Backcountry

Coming into the Valley is an otherworldly experience. Seeing El Capitan around that first bend, Half Dome in the distance, it gives you a sense of reverence. I never used that word because I never could comprehend the emotion until now. Reverence for El Capitan.

Nicholas Trieste

That first ray of light on the Dawn Wall. Similar to a moment walking alone and a joyful memory reflects through your mind, or a simple joke. You'd smile to yourself, and the world around ceases to exist while time lazily drifts onward. That moment is frozen and captured never to be repeated the same way, yet as the memory sticks with you forever, so does the first sunrise on El Capitan, just as the first sunset hitting the granite stays forever. Utmost respect, purity and joy.

Betta Fish and Backcountry

I have glossed into that foreign land
where time slows
and dreams hang like dew drops
above a lake of clouds.

Nicholas Trieste

The red moon hangs
With the blood of burnt pine.
Ashes fall like snow.

Betta Fish and Backcountry

"Half Dome"

I have climbed
Let the clouds rest below me
Felt the sting of rocks tearing through
the bottoms of my feet
If only to reach the summit
And shake hands with old gods

Nicholas Trieste

My father's mother
Loved butterflies
He commented on seeing them at her
funeral
I wonder if he loved them the same
Hundreds guiding me through Yosemite

Betta Fish and Backcountry

Lost a toenail today. Or had to peel it off. Either way, it's not there. Have no feeling in the big toe on my left foot. Clinic says it'll come back in a few days when the muscles relax. Shouldn't have nerve damage. I don't care either way. If this is the cost of the 24 miles I've hiked yesterday, I will gladly do it again. I would go through that pure exhaustion, as the cold sun hung above me wandering the mountainside. Contemplating it now, I don't understand how people have no appreciation for the wilderness. It is pure, and it gives, always, whereas we only take, and take, and take. Even the faux-environmentalists on the internet. I wish they'd all come out here, leave their phones, wander, and listen to the sounds around them rather than making everything a photo op.

Nicholas Trieste

Headlamps on El Cap
Fireflies in the night
—twinkling stars

Betta Fish and Backcountry

Cold. Fingers not working right. Writing difficult. I've tucked myself into my mummy bag, stuffed my sweater into the small opening for my face to try and keep as much heat in here as possible. Sleep comes in spurts of thirty-minute stretches. Dreams vivid. Snow falls frequently.

Nicholas Trieste

I lay in a hotel room
Wondering what the chances are that
Friday
And
Next Friday
Are playing on a Saturday
The week I think I found my father
In a group of butterflies
Guiding me through a National Park.
If the Universe
Is a series
Of inconspicuous events
It's doing a very poor job.

Betta Fish and Backcountry

I feel like myself outdoors. There remains little in the way of me being able to talk to people, or not. We either share the same interest out here, say "hello," wave and pass by, or we don't. I have barely been back in modern society for seven hours; it has already become cumbersome: this social distortion of fake smiles and ritualistic arrogance. It was simple out there in Yosemite. Freezing, eating apples and whatever produce I could get for the day. It was simple tucking myself into a sleeping bag at 9 to drift off with the sound of dying leaves as they hit the side of my tent. Now I lay awake, wishing that I never came home to insomnia. True joy lies in the wilderness, searching for the next adventure, meeting the same souls who strive for the peace we have lost.

Nicholas Trieste

She was warm sugar
in the fall air

Betta Fish and Backcountry

Standing,
Formless,
Fingertips on the windowsill
Collecting dust

Nicholas Trieste

The purples
Mix with hues of pink
Across an atrophied landscape
Realization that the world is sleeping

Betta Fish and Backcountry

Dream in black and white
Revelations of days gone
When time slowed
And for a moment
It all felt perfect

Nicholas Trieste

"This life is inescapable"

Dream of memories
Nostalgic   depression   for   morning
breakfast

Betta Fish and Backcountry

Give your life
To the dark embrace
Accept that finality of it all
So you may live

"Late January, 3:12 am."

Let the winter wind howl
Among the dead branches
Where leaves once clung:
Their rustling a melody
Lost in the snow.

Betta Fish and Backcountry

Alaskan Native said
People who come here
Are chasing something
Or running from it.

Nicholas Trieste

Walk off into the wilderness
Sit at the edge of a glacier
Watch as the moose pass by

Betta Fish and Backcountry

As I watched the wilderness engulf me, I began to wonder if I was making the right choices: if my foot placement was perfect on slippery rock; if tree branches would hold my weight as I began to descend; if I would find the necessities of what I longed for while alone in the backcountry. To be purposefully lost far from home in a state I had no friends, or relatives, without service, and only what I could carry on my back as comfort. What an adventure! a first for feeling alive.

Nicholas Trieste

"Sunset"

The glow radiates,
creates an orange half-globe behind the
mountains.
The sun picks up a redeye on the ridge
as it drifts lazily
to wake up the other side of the planet.

Betta Fish and Backcountry

I'm turning 27 this year. If I died the same age as my father, my life would already be half over. To think all of the things he missed out on without even knowing his time was ticking away so quickly. Would we all change if we could see the time we had left, a watch on our wrist with the exact amount of days, minutes, and seconds?

Nicholas Trieste

"Campfire Will"

Do not bury me
when the hunter comes to butcher my body
with the long blade
he sharpened
while watching the fog roll in on the
dawn.

Let the buzzards pick my eyes clean:
make new caves for the mice to call home,
and for the wolves,
I leave my ligaments
to clean between their teeth.

My heart belongs to the Earth:
the least I could give to Nature
for showing me love.